Animal Top Tens

Europe's Most Amazing Animals

Anita Ganeri

Raintree

www.raintreepublishers.co.uk
Visit our website to find out more information about Raintree books.

To order:
☎ Phone 44 (0) 1865 888112
📄 Send a fax to 44 (0) 1865 314091
💻 Visit the Raintree Bookshop at www.raintreepublishers.co.uk to browse our catalogue and order online

Raintree is an imprint of Capstone Global Library Limited, a company incorporated in England and Wales having its registered office at 7 Pilgrim Street, London, EC4V 6LB – Registered company number: 6695582

Editorial: Nancy Dickmann and Catherine Veitch
Design: Victoria Bevan and Geoff Ward
Illustrations: Geoff Ward
Picture Research: Mica Brancic
Production: Victoria Fitzgerald

Originated by Modern Age
Printed and bound by CTPS (China Translation & Printing Services Ltd)

13-digit ISBN 978 1 4062 0917 4 (hardback)
12 11 10 09 08
10 9 8 7 6 5 4 3 2 1

13-digit ISBN 978 1 4062 0927 3 (paperback)
13 12 11 10 09
10 9 8 7 6 5 4 3 2 1

British Library Cataloguing in Publication Data
Ganeri, Anita, 1961-
    Europe's Most Amazing Animals.
(Animal top tens)
    591.9'4
A full catalogue record for this book is available from the British Library

Acknowledgements
The author and publisher are grateful to the following for permission to reproduce copyright material: ©Alamy/blickwinkel/Hecker p. **14**; ©Ardea pp. **4** (Steffen & Alexandra Sailer), **6** (John Cancalosi), **7** (Stefan Meyers), **8** (Pascal Goetgheluck), **12** (Duncan Usher), **21** (Piers Cavendish); ©FLPA pp. **11** (Derek Middleton), **19** (Chris Mattison), **20** (Jurgen & Christine Sohns); ©FLPA/Foto Natura Stock p. **25**; ©FLPA/Minden Pictures/JH Editorial p. **17** (Cyril Ruoso); Naturepl p. **10** (Dietmar Nill) [OSF]; ©OSF pp. **16** (Juniors Bildarchiv), **18** (Mike Linley), **22** (Manfred Pfefferle), **23** (Emanuele Biggi), **24** (Rodger Jackman), **27** (Antinolo Jorge Sierra); ©OSF/Mauritius Die Bildagentur Gmbh pp. **9** (Rauschenbach), **15** (DHerrmann Dherrmann), **26** (Pölking Pölking); ©OSF/Robert Harding Picture Library Ltd p. **13** (Steve & Ann Toon).

Cover photograph of a European eagle owl, reproduced with permission of PhotoLibrary/Juniors Bildarchiv.

The publishers would like to thank Michael Bright for his assistance with the preparation of this book.

Every effort has been made to contact copyright holders of any material reproduced in this book. Any omissions will be rectified in subsequent printings if notice is given to the publishers.

Contents

Some words are printed in bold, **like this**. You can find out what they mean on page 31 in the Glossary.

Europe

Europe is the second smallest **continent**, covering just over 10,000,000 sq kilometres (3,860,000 sq miles). Only Australasia is smaller than Europe. It stretches from Spain and Portugal in the west, to Russia in the east. To the north there is Scandinavia. To the south there is the Mediterranean Sea.

Europe has many different kinds of landscape. A curve of mountains roughly divides the cooler north from the warmer south. Huge forests of fir and pine trees stretch across the far north. Further south are large grassy open spaces, mountains and **woodlands**. Around the Mediterranean Sea, the weather is hot and dry.

Woodlands of **broadleaved** trees are home to many animals.

N
W—E
S

Iceland

Atlantic Ocean

North
Sea

Scandinavia

Baltic
Sea

Russia

British Isles

Denmark

E U R O P E

Alps

River Danube

Black Sea

Portugal

Spain

Key
forest
mountains
— river

0   500 miles
0   500 kilometres

Mediterranean Sea

An amazing range of animals has **adapted** to live in these
different **habitats**. Birds, deer, and wild cats live around
the River Danube where it flows into the sea. The forests
are home to wood ants and many kinds of birds. Goats
and rare brown bears live in the mountains of southern
Europe. These animals all have special features to help
them survive in their particular homes.

Wild boar

The wild boar is a large pig, with dark brown, bristly hair. It is active at **dawn** and **dusk** when it searches for food. It uses its long snout to search among the leaves on the forest floor for nuts, **fungi**, roots, mice, and snails.

WILD BOAR

BODY LENGTH:
1.5–1.8 M (4.9–5.9 FT)

WEIGHT:
50–200 KG
(110–440 LBS)

LIFESPAN:
15–20 YEARS

HABITAT:
WOODLANDS

THAT'S AMAZING!:
WILD BOAR LOVE TO WALLOW IN MUD POOLS. THEY DO THIS TO COOL DOWN AND GET RID OF IRRITATING **INSECTS**.

■ where wild boar live

North Sea

Atlantic Ocean

Europe

Mediterranean Sea

Male boars have two upward-pointing tusks which are extra-large teeth.

Wild boar use sounds, such as grunts and squeals, to communicate.

Woodlands

Temperate woodlands grow in places which have warm summers and mild winters. The trees are mostly broadleaved trees such as oak, beech, and silver birch. They are mostly deciduous which means that they lose their leaves in winter.

Family groups

Wild boar piglets are born in a den under a pile of rocks or a fallen tree. The piglets have brown and cream stripes to **camouflage** them among the trees. They live with their mothers and other females and their young. These large groups are called 'sounders'.

Stag beetle

The stag beetle is the largest beetle in Europe. It lives among oak, ash, and elm trees. Males use their jaws in fights with other males when they are trying to find a female to **mate** with. The loser gets tipped upside down on to its back. It pushes itself the right way up, then runs away.

STAG BEETLE

BODY LENGTH:
2.5–7.5 CM (0.9–2.9 IN)

WEIGHT:
ABOUT 2 G (0.07 OZ)

LIFESPAN:
UP TO 7 YEARS

HABITAT:
WOODLANDS

THAT'S AMAZING!:
A STAG BEETLE'S GIANT JAWS ARE USELESS FOR CHEWING. IT SEEMS THAT ADULT BEETLES DO NOT EAT ANYTHING AT ALL.

where stag beetles live

North Sea

Atlantic Ocean

Europe

Mediterranean Sea

This **insect** gets its name from the male's huge jaws, which look like a deer's antlers.

8

Life cycle

Stag beetles live in **woodlands**. They need a good supply of dead wood. The female lays her eggs in rotting logs or the stumps of dead trees. When the **larvae** hatch, they feed on the dead wood. They have strong jaws for tearing and chewing. But the wood does not contain many **nutrients** to help the larvae grow. It takes larvae up to seven years to become adults.

Two male stag beetles about to lock jaws in a fight.

Noctule bat

The noctule bat is one of the largest bats in Europe. It has short, reddish-brown fur, and wide, triangular wings. Noctule bats live in **woodlands** where there are hollow trees. They use the trees for roosting, raising their young and **hibernating**. They leave their roosts at **dusk** to search for moths, beetles, and other flying **insects**, which they catch in the air and eat.

NOCTULE BAT

BODY LENGTH:
6–8 CM (2.3–3.1 IN)

WEIGHT:
18–40 G (0.6–1.4 OZ)

LIFESPAN:
UP TO 12 YEARS

HABITAT:
WOODLANDS

THAT'S AMAZING!:
A BABY NOCTULE BAT CAN FLY WHEN IT IS FOUR WEEKS OLD.

■ where noctule bats live

North Sea

Atlantic Ocean

Europe

Mediterranean Sea

Noctule bats fly fast and high above the ground.

Winter sleep

In winter, when the weather is cold and there isn't much to eat, some bats in Europe fly to warmer places further south. Others find a tree hole and fall into a deep sleep, called hibernation. During hibernation, the bats sometimes sit on top of each other for warmth.

In summer, noctule bats roost in holes in hollow trees.

Migration
Many animals make long journeys between their breeding and feeding grounds. This is called migration. It lets them take advantage of the best weather and food supplies.

European eagle owl

The eagle owl is the largest owl in Europe. It lives in open **woodland** with rocky areas. It roosts in the trees during the day and makes its nest in cracks in the rocks. The eagle owl has a large beak, enormous **talons**, bright orange eyes, and long, fluffy ear tufts.

EUROPEAN EAGLE OWL

BODY LENGTH:
70 CM (27.3 IN)

WEIGHT:
4 KG (8.8 LBS)

LIFESPAN:
UP TO 40 YEARS

HABITAT:
WOODLANDS, ROCKY AREAS

THAT'S AMAZING!:
HOURS AFTER AN OWL HAS EATEN A MEAL, IT SICKS UP A PARCEL OF BONES AND OTHER BITS OF ITS PREY THAT IT CANNOT DIGEST.

where European eagle owls live

North Sea

Atlantic Ocean

Europe

Mediterranean Sea

The owl's large eyes help it to find its prey at night.

The owl's wings are fringed with feathers to help it fly silently.

Forest hunter

The eagle owl is a powerful **predator**. It searches for **prey** at **dusk** and in the early evening. It kills woodland animals, from small deer to mice. It swoops down on its victim, grabs it in its talons and flies off with it in its beak. Small animals are swallowed whole. Larger animals are torn apart. The eagle owl has superb eyesight and hearing for finding its prey in the dark.

Alpine salamander

The Alpine salamander is a shiny black **amphibian**. It lives in mountain forests and spends the day hiding in **burrows** or cracks in the rocks. At night, it leaves its hiding place to search for beetles, spiders, and centipedes to eat.

ALPINE SALAMANDER

BODY LENGTH:
9–14 CM (3.5–5.4 IN)

WEIGHT:
15 G (0.5 OZ)

LIFESPAN:
10 YEARS

HABITAT:
MOUNTAINS

THAT'S AMAZING!:
TO AVOID THE COLD WEATHER AND LACK OF FOOD IN WINTER, ALPINE SALAMANDERS **HIBERNATE** FOR 6–8 MONTHS OF THE YEAR.

where alpine salamanders live

North Sea

Atlantic Ocean

Europe

Mediterranean Sea

The Alpine salamander lives at heights of up to 3,000 metres (9,840 feet) in the Alps.

Young Alpine salamanders look like miniature versions of their parents.

Mountain survival

The Alpine salamander has some very unusual features to help it survive in the cold, dry mountains. Most amphibians lay eggs in the water. The eggs hatch into fish-like tadpoles. Alpine salamanders give birth to live young. This means that their young avoid the danger of their pond freezing over or drying out. The young stay inside their mother for up to three years before they are born. This protects them from the harsh conditions and also from **predators**.

Alpine marmot

Alpine marmots are large squirrels that live in the mountains of central and southern Europe. The marmots are active during the day, when they mostly feed on grass, flowers, seeds, and bulbs.

An Alpine marmot has thick fur, a short tail, and small ears.

ALPINE MARMOT

BODY LENGTH:
53–73 CM (20–28 IN)

WEIGHT:
4–8 KG (8.8–17.6 LBS)

LIFESPAN:
4–5 YEARS

HABITAT:
MOUNTAINS

THAT'S AMAZING!:
ALPINE MARMOTS TELL EACH OTHER OF DANGER, SUCH AS EAGLES OR FOXES NEARBY, BY WHISTLING A WARNING.

■ where alpine marmots live

North Sea

Atlantic Ocean

Europe

Mediterranean Sea

Winter sleep

In summer, Alpine marmots eat as much food as possible. Then they spend 6 or 7 months **hibernating**, huddling together for warmth. The last marmot in the **burrow** plugs up the entrance with earth and droppings to keep out the cold. The marmots live off their stores of fat until spring comes.

Alpine marmots live in burrows, which they dig out with their strong paws and claws.

Hibernation

Winter is a hard time for animals. The weather is cold and food is scarce. Some animals survive by hibernating. Their body temperature drops, and their heart and breathing rates slow down. They sleep very deeply until the weather gets warmer in spring.

Mallorcan midwife toad

The Mallorcan midwife toad lives in the mountains of northern Mallorca (an island off the east coast of Spain). It is well **adapted** to the difficult conditions. Its body is flat so that it can squeeze into cracks in the rocks where it hides during the day. It comes out at night to feed on **insects** which it catches with its long, sticky tongue.

The toad's golden-coloured skin provides good **camouflage**.

MIDWIFE TOAD

BODY LENGTH:
UP TO 38 MM (1.4 IN)

LIFESPAN:
10 YEARS

HABITAT:
MOUNTAINS

THAT'S AMAZING!:
THE TOAD'S BACK
IS COVERED IN
SMALL WARTS. THE
WARTS GIVE OFF A
STRONG-SMELLING
POISON IF THE TOAD
IS ATTACKED.

where midwife toads live

North Sea

Atlantic Ocean

Europe

Mallorca

Mediterranean Sea

The male toad carries the eggs until they hatch to protect them from **predators**.

Caring parents

Midwife toads are unusual because the male toad looks
after the eggs. The female lays strings of eggs which the
male wraps around his back legs. When the eggs are ready
to hatch, the male wades into the water and lets the tadpoles
jump out. Water is rare in the toad's **habitat** but this
makes sure that the tadpoles have a pool to grow in.

Peregrine

The peregrine is a crow-sized bird with long, pointed wings and a short tail. Males have grey backs with striped chests. Females are larger and darker. The peregrine lives in **moorland** and along rocky coasts. It lays its eggs in hollow trees or on rocky ledges. Its **habitat** provides it with plenty of open space for finding **prey**.

Falcons have strong, hooked beaks.

PEREGRINE

BODY LENGTH:
34–50 CM (13.2–19.5 IN)

WEIGHT:
0.5–1.5 KG (1.1–3.3 LBS)

LIFESPAN:
15 YEARS

HABITAT:
MOORLAND;
ROCKY SEA COASTS

THAT'S AMAZING!:
PEREGRINES **MATE** FOR LIFE AND
RETURN TO THE SAME NESTING
SITE YEAR AFTER YEAR.

where peregrines live

North
Sea

Atlantic
Ocean

Europe

Mediterranean Sea

The way the peregrine dives down on prey is called stooping.

Speedy flier

The peregrine is a high-speed **predator**. When it is chasing prey in the air, it can reach speeds of up to 200 kilometres (124 miles) per hour. This makes it one of the fastest flying birds. It mostly feeds on other birds, such as pigeons. It spots its prey from a distance, then closes its wings and dives down for the kill.

Grass snake

Grass snakes live in damp places, such as grassy river banks, ditches, and ponds. They are well **adapted** to their **habitat**. The snake's skin is grey-green with black and yellow markings. This **camouflages** it among the long grass. The snake is a very good swimmer and searches for its **prey** of tadpoles, frogs, and fish in the water.

A grass snake usually swims with its head out of the water.

GRASS SNAKE

BODY LENGTH:
70–120 CM (27.3–46.8 IN)

WEIGHT:
90–300 G (3.1–10.5 OZ)

LIFESPAN:
UP TO 15 YEARS

HABITAT:
RIVER BANKS, PONDS, DITCHES

THAT'S AMAZING!:
GRASS SNAKES **HIBERNATE** FROM OCTOBER TO MARCH UNDER TREE ROOTS OR IN OLD RABBIT **BURROWS**.

■ where grass snakes live

North Sea

Atlantic Ocean

Europe

Mediterranean Sea

A grass snake can play dead for half an hour or more.

Grass snake defences

Grass snakes are eaten by badgers, foxes, and hedgehogs.
If a snake is in danger, it puffs up its body and hisses
loudly to frighten off its attacker. If this does not work,
it squirts out a foul-smelling liquid. If this also fails, the
snake rolls over on to its back and pretends to be dead.
It stays completely still with its mouth open and its
tongue hanging out until its attacker loses interest.

European eel

European eels are long, narrow fish that spend part of their lives in the sea and part in rivers. They make an extraordinary journey between their two **habitats**.

EUROPEAN EEL

BODY LENGTH:
20–80 CM (7.87–31.2 IN)

WEIGHT:
UP TO 6.5 KG (14.3 LBS)

LIFESPAN:
85 YEARS

HABITAT:
RIVERS; SEA

THAT'S AMAZING!:
ON THEIR LONG JOURNEY, THE EELS CAN SURVIVE FOR SEVERAL HOURS OUT OF THE WATER SO THAT THEY CAN TRAVEL OVERLAND.

where European eels live

North Sea

Atlantic Ocean

Europe

Mediterranean Sea

Young eels are called glass eels because their bodies are see-through.

Eel lives

An eel lays its eggs in the Sargasso Sea, in the Atlantic Ocean. The eggs hatch into **larvae** which look like curled leaves. For up to three years, they drift on the ocean currents towards the coast. Then they turn into young eels that swim up rivers and spend up to 20 years growing into adults. As adults, they travel thousands of kilometres back to the sea to lay their eggs.

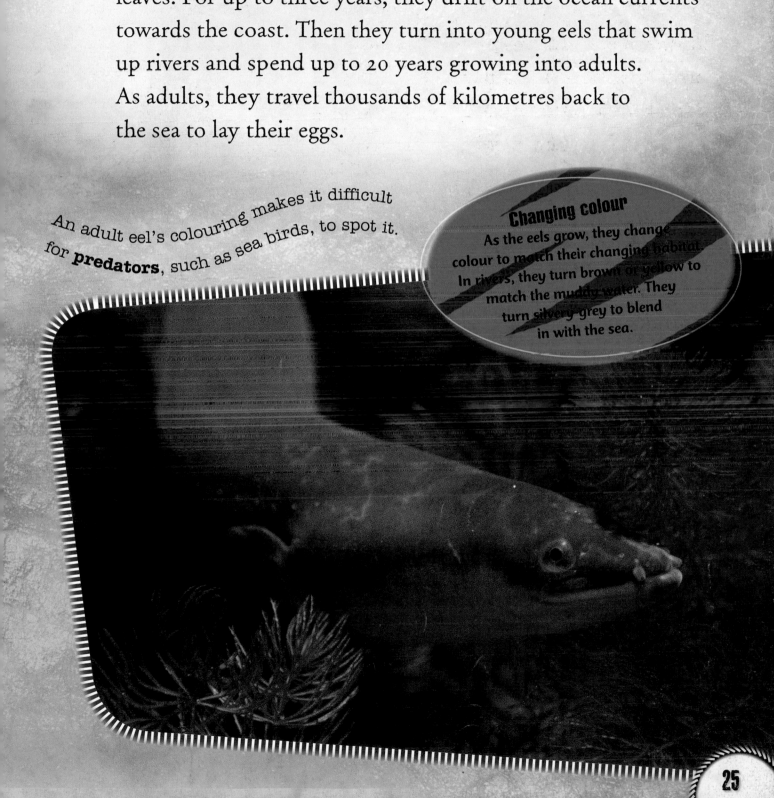

An adult eel's colouring makes it difficult for **predators**, such as sea birds, to spot it.

Changing colour

As the eels grow, they change colour to match their changing habitat. In rivers, they turn brown or yellow to match the muddy water. They turn silvery-grey to blend in with the sea.

Animals in danger

Many animals in Europe are in danger of dying out. When an animal dies out, it is said to be **extinct**. Many animals are dying out because people are destroying their **habitats**, capturing them for pets, or killing them for their skins, meat, and body parts.

The osprey is a rare **bird of prey** that lives near lakes, rivers, and the sea. In the past, ospreys were shot by fish farmers because the birds ate the farmers' fish. Their nest sites were also destroyed and their eggs stolen by egg collectors. Today, ospreys are being reintroduced to specially protected nesting sites and their numbers are growing.

Ospreys feed mainly on fish. They plunge into the water to catch prey.

The Spanish lynx used to be found throughout Spain and Portugal. It now only lives in a few forests in southern Spain. Much of its habitat has been destroyed to make room for building homes and hotels. The lynx hunts wild rabbits but many rabbits are being killed by disease. This is another threat to the lynx.

Today, **conservation** groups are working hard to save these amazing animals.

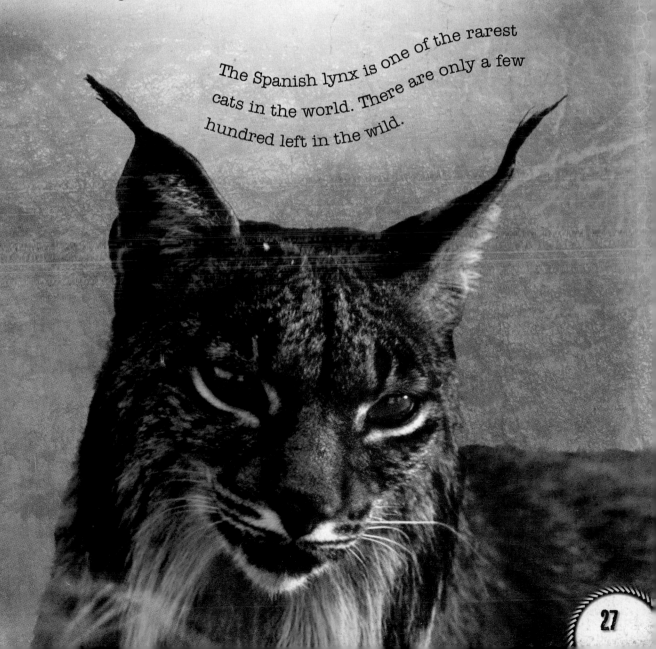

The Spanish lynx is one of the rarest cats in the world. There are only a few hundred left in the wild.

Animal facts and figures

There are millions of different kinds of animals living all over the world. The place where an animal lives is called its **habitat**. Animals have special features, such as wings, claws, and fins. These features allow animals to survive in their habitats. Which animal do you think is the most amazing?

WILD BOAR

BODY LENGTH:
1.5–1.8 M (4.9–5.9 FT)

WEIGHT:
50–200 KG (110–440 LBS)

LIFESPAN:
15–20 YEARS

HABITAT:
WOODLANDS

THAT'S AMAZING!:
WILD BOAR LOVE TO WALLOW IN MUD POOLS. THEY DO THIS TO COOL DOWN AND GET RID OF IRRITATING **INSECTS**.

STAG BEETLE

BODY LENGTH:
2.5–7.5 CM (0.9–2.9 IN)

WEIGHT:
ABOUT 2 G (0.07 OZ)

LIFESPAN:
UP TO 7 YEARS

HABITAT:
WOODLANDS

THAT'S AMAZING!:
A STAG BEETLE'S GIANT JAWS ARE USELESS FOR CHEWING AND IT SEEMS THAT ADULT BEETLES DO NOT EAT ANYTHING AT ALL.

NOCTULE BAT

BODY LENGTH:
6–8 CM (2.3–3.1 IN)

WEIGHT:
18–40 G (0.6–1.4 OZ)

LIFESPAN:
UP TO 12 YEARS

HABITAT:
WOODLANDS

THAT'S AMAZING!:
A BABY NOCTULE BAT CAN FLY WHEN IT IS FOUR WEEKS OLD.

EUROPEAN EAGLE OWL

BODY LENGTH:
70 CM (27.3 IN)

WEIGHT:
4 KG (8.8 LBS)

LIFESPAN:
UP TO 40 YEARS

HABITAT:
WOODLANDS, ROCKY AREAS

THAT'S AMAZING!:
HOURS AFTER AN OWL HAS EATEN A MEAL, IT SICKS UP A PARCEL OF BONES AND OTHER BITS OF ITS PREY THAT IT CANNOT DIGEST.

ALPINE SALAMANDER

BODY LENGTH:
9–14 CM (3.5–5.4 IN)

WEIGHT:
15 G (0.5 OZ)

LIFESPAN:
10 YEARS

HABITAT:
MOUNTAINS

THAT'S AMAZING!:
TO AVOID THE COLD WEATHER AND LACK OF FOOD IN WINTER, ALPINE SALAMANDERS **HIBERNATE** FOR 6–8 MONTHS OF THE YEAR.

ALPINE MARMOT

BODY LENGTH:
53–73 CM (20–28 IN)

WEIGHT:
4–8 KG (8.8–17.6 LBS)

LIFESPAN:
4–5 YEARS

HABITAT:
MOUNTAINS

THAT'S AMAZING!:
ALPINE MARMOTS TELL EACH OTHER OF DANGER, SUCH AS EAGLES OR FOXES NEARBY, BY WHISTLING A WARNING.

MIDWIFE TOAD

BODY LENGTH:
UP TO 38 MM (1.4 IN)

LIFESPAN:
10 YEARS

HABITAT:
MOUNTAINS

THAT'S AMAZING!:
THE TOAD'S BACK IS COVERED IN SMALL WARTS WHICH GIVE OFF A STRONG-SMELLING POISON IF THE TOAD IS ATTACKED.

PEREGRINE

BODY LENGTH:
34–50 CM (13.2–19.5 IN)

WEIGHT:
0.5–1.5 KG (1.1–3.3 LBS)

LIFESPAN:
15 YEARS

HABITAT:
MOORLAND; ROCKY SEA COASTS

THAT'S AMAZING!:
PEREGRINES **MATE** FOR LIFE AND RETURN TO THE SAME NESTING SITE YEAR AFTER YEAR.

GRASS SNAKE

BODY LENGTH:
70–120 CM (27.3–46.8 IN)

WEIGHT:
90–300 G (3.1–10.5 OZ)

LIFESPAN:
UP TO 15 YEARS

HABITAT:
RIVER BANKS, PONDS, DITCHES

THAT'S AMAZING!:
GRASS SNAKES HIBERNATE FROM OCTOBER TO MARCH UNDER TREE ROOTS OR IN OLD RABBIT **BURROWS**.

EUROPEAN EEL

BODY LENGTH:
20–80 CM (7.87–31.2 IN)

WEIGHT:
UP TO 6.5 KG (14.3 LBS)

LIFESPAN:
85 YEARS

HABITAT:
RIVERS; SEA

THAT'S AMAZING!:
ON THEIR LONG JOURNEY, THE EELS CAN SURVIVE FOR SEVERAL HOURS OUT OF THE WATER SO THAT THEY CAN TRAVEL OVERLAND.

Find out more

Books to read

Exploring Continents: Europe, Jane Bingham (Heinemann
   Library, 2007)

Living Things: Adaptation, Holly Wallace (Heinemann Library, 2001)

Living Things: Survival and Change, Holly Wallace (Heinemann
   Library, 2001)

Websites

http://www.bbc.co.uk/nature/reallywild
   Type in the name of the animal you want to learn about
   and find a page with lots of facts, figures, and pictures.

http://animals.nationalgeographic.com/animals
   This site has information on the different groups of animals, stories
   of survival in different habitats, and stunning photo galleries to
   search through.

http://animaldiversity.ummz.umich.edu
   A website run by the University of Michigan which has
   a huge encyclopedia of animals to search through.

http://www.mnh.si.edu
   The website of the Smithsonian National Museum of Natural History,
   which has one of the largest natural history collections in the world.

Zoo sites
   Many zoos around the world have their own websites which
   tell you about the animals they keep, where they come from,
   and how they are looked after.

Glossary

adapted when an animal has special features that help it to survive in its habitat

amphibian animal, such as a toad or frog, that lives both on land and in the water

bird of prey bird that hunts for food using its talons

broadleaved trees, such as oaks and elms, that have wide leaves

burrow hole in the ground or in a tree where an animal shelters

camouflage when an animal has special colours or markings which help to hide it in its habitat

conservation saving and protecting wild animals and their habitats

continent one of seven huge pieces of land on Earth. Each continent is divided into smaller regions called countries.

dawn when the sun rises in the morning

dusk when the sun sets in the evening

extinct when a kind of animal dies out forever

fungi mushrooms, toadstools and moulds

habitat place where an animal lives and feeds

hibernate to go into a deep sleep over winter

insect animal with six legs and three parts to its body

larvae grub-like young of insects

mate when an animal makes babies with another animal

moorland rocky habitat covered in low-growing plants, such as heather

nutrient substance found in the environment that animals need to grow and survive

predator animal that hunts and kills other animals for food

prey animal that is hunted and killed by other animals for food

talon bird's large, curved claw

woodland forest in which the trees are mostly broadleaved and deciduous (lose their leaves in winter)

Index